P9-ARN-502

•

CHILDPROOFING
YOUR
HOME

•

Childproofing ●
Your ●
Home ●

Arlene Stewart

Illustrated by Claude Martinot

WITHDRAWN

T.X
150
.S74
1984

LEARNING RESOURCE CENTER
CHARLES COUNTY COMMUNITY COLLEGE
LA PLATA, MARYLAND

048523

Addison-Wesley Publishing Company
Reading, Massachusetts • Menlo Park, California
London • Amsterdam • Don Mills, Ontario • Sydney

For my safety-conscious husband,
Mark Levine

Library of Congress Cataloging in Publication Data

Stewart, Arlene.
  Childproofing your home.

  1. Home accidents — Prevention. 2. Children's
accidents — Prevention. I. Title.

TX150.S74 1984   649'.1'0289   83-25845
ISBN 0-201-07888-0

Copyright © 1984 by Arlene Stewart

All rights reserved. No part of this publication may be re-
produced, stored in a retrieval system, or transmitted, in
any form or by any means, electronic, mechanical, photo-
copying, recording, or otherwise, without the prior written
permission of the publisher. Printed in the United States of
America. Published simultaneously in Canada.

Designed by Larry Kazal K.C. Witherell, New York
Set in 10 point Times Roman by Wendy B. Wolf

ISBN 0-201-07888-0

ABCDEFGHIJ-AL-87654
First printing, February 1984

Contents

CONTENTS

2 Trouble Spots in the Home 32

3 Poison Alert 40

CONTENTS

INTRODUCTION

Before I had my daughter Annalee, I never realized all the dangers around me — medicine cabinets filled with poisons, hot stoves and fireplaces, sharp edges on coffee tables and furniture. Every room held peril I had never before imagined: bookcases that Annalee could pull over, hot drinks I got to one second before she did, telephone cords as threatening as a hangman's noose. Keeping on top of everything seemed overwhelming, but since then, I've learned that effective childproofing need not be the result of harrowing experiences. If you take the time to childproof in advance and combine it with common sense you can prevent a lot of accidents . . . while encouraging your child to discover the joys of his or her new world.

The ideal time to start childproofing is before your baby is born. Go around the house *now*, while you have time, and safeproof as much as possible. Get down on the floor and look around from your baby's point of view. Those dangling electrical cords look tasty, and so does that bottle of bleach left under the sink. What about those open windows with a twenty-foot drop under them? Try to imagine what might intrigue a small child and you'll be off to a good start.

Always anticipate the different stages of your child's development. Soon you'll find that your safety-proofing strategies will grow with your child. Six-month-olds will be rolling, creeping, crawling, and the first major wave of safety-proofing will be tested. One-year-old walkers see the world from the liberating height of their feet and can't be trusted with anything. And as for young climbers, they're a real threat to parental peace of mind at any age.

INTRODUCTION

Living with a small child requires patience, tremendous organizational skills, and the imagination to anticipate what he or she will get into next. In this book I have gone around the home room-by-room pointing out the most obvious dangers. I've included sections on car safety, baby equipment, and ways to protect your child in playgrounds, and visiting and travel. I've also tried to include suggestions to encourage your child to be independent without being fearful.

Remember that no parent can prevent all accidents. All children get hurt once in a while. Skinned knees and bruises are a part of growing up. So is adventure. The last thing any of us want is to live in a padded cell or shout "No!" hundreds of times a day.

But if something should happen to your child, be prepared by familiarizing yourself with common first aid techniques now. This also applies to any person who watches your child in your absence. Discuss emergency procedures with everyone with whom you leave your child, including friends and relatives. Leave a letter authorizing emergency medical treatment that may be necessary in the event you can't be reached.

Our hope, then, is that we make our world safe enough for our children to explore with confidence and joy.

1

Childproofing Room-by-Room

The kitchen

This is the room you'll be in the most! Make it fun by making it safe. Small infants soon become inquisitive toddlers eager to "help" Mom and Dad. Unfortunately, the kitchen contains many potential hazards that you must anticipate before your baby gets to them ... hot stoves, sharp utensils,

Pot and pan handles should be turned toward the back of the stove.

poisonous cleansers, and more. (Having a baby will be a good opportunity to reorganize your shelves and utensils anyway!) Start in advance and look around with a keen baby-level eye.

Stoves: *Teach your child never to touch the stove — whether you're cooking or not.*

▶ When cooking always turn the handles of pans and skillets inward to prevent tipping and accidental spills.

▶ Fry or boil foods on the back burners to reduce splatter.

▶ Never take hot pans out of the oven and leave in reach of the baby.

▶ Check the insulation of oven doors. Turn on the oven; if the door is hot to the touch, keep the baby away. Many small hands have been burned when Mom and Dad failed to notice this.

▶ Always turn off oven and burners after use.

▶ Cover burners on electric stoves after using.

▶ Install dry chemical fire extinguishers, placed safely away from your baby, to put out electric, grease, and ordinary fires.

▶ To reduce distractions, try to cook when your baby is not underfoot.
Never leave your child alone in the kitchen.

Pot and pan storage

▶ If your oven has a storage area for pots and pans, organize it by placing the heaviest objects on the bottom to reduce the chance of an avalanche on the baby.

▶ Also check for insulation here; if pots and pans get hot, consider a lock for the oven door.

▶ Move all breakable equipment to high shelves along with anything that has sharp edges — graters, components for food processors, blades, etc.

▶ Install childproof locks on the inside of all utensil drawers and cupboards. Several brands are available in hardware stores. These plastic safety latches allow an adult to open the drawer wide enough to slip fingers in and release the safety hook from latch. Latches are also available which slide through handles or knobs to keep doors locked.

Under the sink: Storing Cleaning Agents

Most of us acquire household cleaning products with abandon before the baby is born. *It's important for you to inventory all your cleaners now.*

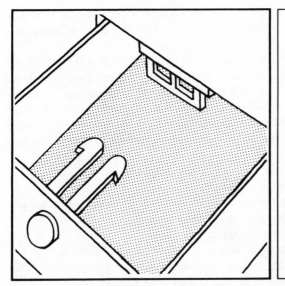

One type of safety latch available. An adult can release the safety mechanism in a drawer lock but a child can't.

Many of these products are deadly. Many more can cause serious injury if ingested accidentally by your baby. Look at everything you have; ask yourself if you really use these products and get rid of what you don't need. Anything you do keep, store in a high place, not in cabinets under the sink that your baby could easily get to.

soap powders,
including dishwashing detergents
bleach
wall cleansers
floor waxes
scouring powders
ammonia and ammonia cleansers
carpet cleaners
drain cleaners
metal polishes
furniture polishes

spot removers
lubricant oils
insecticides
furniture polish
dusting products
wax removers
mothballs
laundry pre-soak
oven cleaners
window cleaners
shoe polish

Read the labels on all household products you store. Many are flammable at high temperatures. Never store anything without a label — in case of an accident, you or your babysitter must know how to act fast! (See Poisons, p.41.)

Garbage areas: With a child in your home, garbage will multiply at a breathtaking rate. Often, in today's small living spaces, we have little choice as to where the garbage will be located. It's best to keep garbage cans away from the baby — under the sink (fitted with a babyproof lock), or on the back porch. If you're forced to keep garbage out in the open where the baby has access to it, *teach your baby never to touch garbage cans or wastepaper baskets.*

And to be safety-wise you should:

> ▸ *Always* cover garbage containers with babyproof lids. Avoid swinging tops that can catch little fingers.
> ▸ Make sure the can is toppleproof.
> ▸ Don't encourage your baby to "help" throw away garbage.
> ▸ Don't throw sharp objects into garbage without wrapping well. They could protrude from the bag and cut your baby or you.
> ▸ Don't store plastic garbage bags where the baby can play with them. *Keep all plastic bags safely locked up.* This includes shopping bags, Baggies, sandwich bags, plastic food wrap. Babies are irresistibly attracted to them, and plastic bags are very dangerous, as they can cause suffocation.
> ▸ Don't spray or clean cans with aerosol cleaners that contain poisons. The baby could touch residue or inhale fumes.

Floors: Because of a baby's smallness and means of locomotion, floors become of primary importance. To keep them hygienic, nonslippery, and safe:

> ▸ Wipe up all spills immediately, before the baby gets to them.
> ▸ Pick up spilled bits of food immediately; what you forget, your baby will find.
> ▸ Banish all scatter rugs. They can cause tumbles.
> ▸ Try to pick up all toys and playthings for the same reason.
> ▸ Always clean up broken glass immediately with wet paper towels, then vacuum thoroughly. It's tedious but you must pick up glass splinters before your baby does.

▸ Repair curled-up linoleum or loose floor tiles. They can be tripped over and can shelter bits of decaying food.

Hot irons and other appliances: Most people have plenty of electrically powered appliances in their homes.

▸ Always place irons out of the baby's reach after using. Wrap the cord tightly around it so the baby can't yank off counter. Remember that irons retain heat for quite a while after use.

▸ Store ironing board where it can't fall on your child, or catch fingers.

▸ Get into the habit of unplugging after *every use* all coffee grinders, food processors, electric knives, blenders, mixers, waffle irons, ice cream machines, automatic coffee makers and espresso machines, and electric can openers.

▸ If you have an automatic coffee maker, be sure your child can't pull it off the counter or table.

Beware of dangling cords

▸ Never leave cords hanging over counter tops or within your baby's reach.

Keep your appliances as far back as possible from the edge of the counter. Fasten the cords to the wall with insulated staples.

▶ Tack down all excess cord and loose cords from permanently positioned appliances.
▶ Replace frayed cords immediately.

Major appliances: Sometimes major appliances can spell major headaches for the parents of an active child. Try to make them "off-limits" but also look out for:

REFRIGERATORS

▶ *Refrigerator doors* that can shut quickly and trap a baby's fingers
▶ *Breakable glass containers* and messy liquids that can spill over a quick grabber
▶ *Medicines or vitamins* stored within the baby's reach
▶ *Unused refrigerators* or freezers — lock or remove doors so your baby cannot get trapped inside.

DISHWASHERS

Babies love them, as do parents. Load and unload during the baby's nap to lessen distraction. Don't let the baby touch dishwasher detergent, which could be harmful if ingested. Check dishwasher for insulation, and be sure that the baby cannot open the door during hot cycles.

WASHING MACHINES AND DRYERS

Again, make sure your baby cannot turn them on, or crawl in! Watch doors that can pinch little fingers.

MICROWAVE OVENS

Always mount ovens where there is *no* possibility a child can climb up to controls.

Anticipating problems

▶ *Matches* — Make sure they're inaccessible, preferably stored in a difficult-to-open tin.
▶ *Hot liquids* — Keep away from edges of tables and counter tops so the baby can't reach up and grab them.
▶ *Table cloths and placemats* — These are irresistible attractions to be

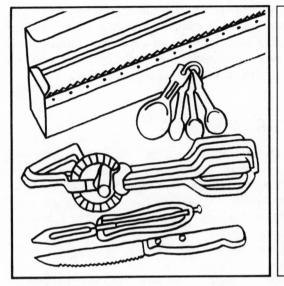

Innocent-looking kitchen items such as boxes of tin foil, egg beaters and measuring spoons have sharp edges that can nick a child's hands.

pulled off tables. Keep hot liquids, sharp utensils, dishes, and china off them when you're not present to supervise.

► *Swinging doors* — Better to remove them entirely than have the baby get hit in the face.

► *Spills* — Wipe them up immediately before you're distracted and slip while carrying your baby.

► *Serrated edges* — On boxes of aluminum foil, plastic wrap, and waxed paper, these sharp edges can cause nasty cuts.

► *Plastic wrappings* — Always dispose of clear plastic wraps, whether they're from vegetables, fruits, or leftovers. The baby can choke on these.

► *Kitchen utensils that can hurt* — Egg beaters, vegetable peelers, metal measuring spoons with sharp edges are potentially dangerous. Check metal rings on plastic spoons which can separate and scratch the baby.

► *Don't let your child sit on the counter tops.* Besides possibly falling off, he or she could reach over and grab something dangerous.

Letting your baby help safely: Give your child his own toys so

that he or she can help cook while you do. Tell him what you're doing as you go along; babies are born mimics and will be happily and safely amused while you get some cooking done. Try to devote a spot in the kitchen that is his or hers alone: a drawer, an accessible shelf in the cupboard, or a box filled with plastic spoons, cups, containers, utensils, and bowls.

Living areas

In today's age of limited housing spaces, your child shares these rooms with Mom and Dad. Many activities are crammed into one space: television, stereo, phone, books, hobbies . . . and now, your baby! You'll soon learn that nothing remains uninteresting to a curious, climbing child. Give your baby freedom to explore, while protecting both child and your other valuables.

Survey your living area now, and look out for:
> ▶ Tipsy floor lamps
> ▶ Sharp edges on coffee tables, bookcases, window sills, furniture arms
> ▶ Poisonous plants and menacing hanging plants that could fall on your baby (see Listing of Poisonous Plants, p.43)
> ▶ Slippery rugs
> ▶ Spindly furniture
> ▶ Glass coffee tables
> ▶ Glass bookshelves and tables
> ▶ Fireplaces (see Fireplaces, p. 37)
> ▶ Unlocked liquor cabinets
> ▶ Empty electric outlets into which the baby can stick fingers, pins, paper clips, small objects
> ▶ Open stairways
> ▶ Marbles or pebbles used in or under planters, which the baby could pick up and swallow
> ▶ Heirlooms, knickknacks, breakables
> ▶ Flower arrangements within the baby's reach
> ▶ Cigars, cigarettes, ashtrays, pipestands
> ▶ Bowls of nuts, popcorn, hard candies
> ▶ Candles

▶ Piles of things that can topple over on your baby: magazines, diaper boxes, books, records, chairs, etc.

▶ Piano keyboard lids that can hurt little fingers

▶ Heavy objects leaning against walls that the baby can pull over: mirrors, artwork, extra chairs, laundry carts, bicycles. (One toddler we know pulled a mirror over onto herself, shattering the glass and cutting herself badly.)

To do now

▶ Replace flimsy furniture with solid pieces that won't topple over when a child climbs on them.

▶ Move all valuables to high shelves.

▶ Move all furniture away from windows so baby has no access.

▶ Install plug protectors in empty sockets, or cover active outlets with plastic outlet covers. These are available in hardware stores and some baby supply stores. (If your baby is a crawler, it's a good idea to take some of these along with you in your diaper bag when visiting friends and relatives.)

▶ Tack down excess electric cords or use cord holders to wind up excess

Keep plastic plug protectors in all outlets. Check behind furniture for outlets you may have forgotten but your child may discover.

cords your baby could play with.

▶ Install plastic corner guards over furniture edges to soften sharp corners. Coffee tables are one of the most hazardous pieces of furniture in your home. They are responsible for countless injuries to young children. Make sure their edges are protected.

▶ Tack down rugs or use nonskid backings to prevent slips and tumbles. Avoid scatter rugs on highly polished floors.

▶ Store or give away any bookcase your growing baby could pull over.

▶ Check that all mirrors and artwork are hung with safety hooks.

▶ Banish all plastic seat covers which could crack and give the baby a cut, or break into little pieces the baby could swallow.

▶ Save your sanity and store any glass furniture — shelves, tables, china closets — until your child is more civilized.

▶ Safety-proof all windows (see Windows, p. 32).

▶ Remove unnecessary extension cords (and keep them out of your baby's reach when in use).

▶ Move all liquor cabinets and storage areas entirely out of a curious baby's reach. It does not require much alcohol to harm your child.

▶ Safety-proof fireplaces (see Fireplaces, p. 37).

Extra electrical cord should be wound onto a cord holder and tucked out of sight.

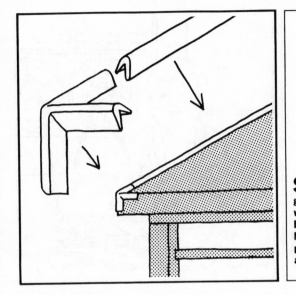

Self-stick plastic corner guards on your coffee table will protect your child from hazardous sharp edges. Many different sizes of plastic guards are available.

Look out for:

THINGS TO KNOCK OVER

> All kinds of heaters (see Sources of Heat, p. 37)
> Humidifiers
> Fans
> Stereo speakers
> Rocking chairs and stools
> Floor lamps

UNSAFE PLACES TO CLIMB INTO

> Toy boxes with heavy lids and no ventilation (see Toys, p. 46)
> Closets
> Armoires
> Chests

Always clean up after an activity or hobby is finished — matches, cigarettes, nail files, sewing kits, games, puzzles, etc. — before you're distracted and your baby discovers them.

Electronic equipment and small children do not mix.

Guarding your expensive stereo and video equipment:
Two approaches work best here:
1. Move everything to high shelves or locked closets.
2. Wait until your child is 18 before buying decent equipment.

Young children are fascinated by stereos, video games, recorders, televisions, tapes, etc. Some older babies and toddlers can be taught to leave equipment alone, but other kids are simply too fascinated to listen. Some parents try to divert this drive by giving their child his or her own toy phonograph, but battery-operated toys are not a good idea until your child is old enough to be taught not to play with batteries (see Toys, p. 46).

Childproof record and book storage: Unless your child's books
and records are jammed tightly in their shelves, you will most likely find yourself picking them up several times a day. Also, heavy books can hurt when they fall on a child's toes. Place them on a high shelf or wedge them in very tightly. Make sure that you don't create stepping stones for the baby with your storage system. (Some parents eliminate bookcases altogether for this reason.)

Do leave a lower bookcase or shelf for the baby's toys and books. Your child will be more satisfied with things he or she can play with, and won't have to hear "No!" all day.

The bathroom

Most babies and young children love bathtime and water play. Early on, we found that our colicky daughter was soothed by a dip in the bathroom sink. As she grew, my husband and I took turns bathing with her in the tub.

Bathtime can be one of the most special of family times. Unfortunately, the bathroom is the room in the house that offers the most opportunities for serious trouble ... slippery floors, dangerous electrical appliances, poisonous cleansers, forbidden medicine cabinets. You'll spend a lot of time in the bathroom, and once toilet training starts, you'll be there even more. Encourage your child to use that bathroom without fear by making it as safe as possible.

The baby-safe medicine cabinet: Review this list of supplies
commonly found in bathrooms. Most of us accumulate so much stuff that we're not even aware of the dangers they pose. Some are mildly toxic, others are deadly poisons. (See Poisons, p.41.) Keep only what you use regularly, and store it high up out of baby's reach. Discard everything else in a garbage can outside the house. *Always read all product labels to familiarize yourself with manufacturer's warnings.*

LOW-TOXICITY PRODUCTS:
> Cosmetics and beauty preparations — cleansing creams, hand lotions, lipstick, skin conditioners, bath oil, toilet water, perfumes, colognes, bubble bath
> Nonmedicated shampoos
> Mercurochrome
> Mineral oil
> Zinc oxide

HIGH-TOXICITY PRODUCTS: Very Harmful
    Hair removers
    Hair dyes, permanent wave solutions, hair straighteners, rinses, hair
        sprays
    Diet pills (amphetamines)
    Shaving supplies — shaving cream, aftershave lotions
    Pharmaceuticals and prescription medicines — aspirin, acetaminophen,
        cough syrups and cold medicines, allergy medicines, sleeping pills,
        laxatives, antidiarrhea medicines, nasal sprays, eye washes, tran-
        quilizers, antidepressants, motion sickness pills
    Denture cleansers
    Contraceptive jellies
    First aid supplies — iodine, hydrogen peroxide, rubbing alcohol (iso-
        propyl)
    Vitamins with iron
    Iron supplement preparations
    Nail polish and polish removers

THINGS TO STORE SAFELY:
    Scissors, nail files, clippers, razor blades

Razor Disposal Note: Always take care disposing of razor blades, and never
throw one away unwrapped — it could cut your baby.

THINGS TO BANISH NOW:
    Old medicines
    Unused medicines
    Any medication without childproof caps

MEDICINE ALERT
If you're like us, your medicine cabinet is probably jammed with prescrip-
tions you were taking for your cold in 1979, or half-used bottles of cough
syrup. Take out all your medicines now and ask yourself if you really need
them. Keep only those that are essential. We recommend that you store them
in a locked container placed on a high shelf in your refrigerator or locked in
your dresser. Consider the following guidelines:

▶ Never keep medicines in anything other than their original containers.

▶ Keep all pill bottles labeled. *In the event of an emergency, you must know what substance your baby has ingested.* (See Poisons, p. 41.)

▶ Never dispense medicines in the dark; you may not give your child the right dosage.

▶ Always follow dosages exactly.

▶ Always discard medicines in their closed childproof containers; flush medicines down the toilet or pour them down the sink.

▶ Never give your child "old" medicines or substitute smaller dosages of adult medicines.

▶ Don't teach your child that medicine is candy even if you're trying to get an important prescription down a balky child's throat. Who would be to blame if he or she drank a bottle of cherry-flavored cough syrup?

▶ If you're ill while you're taking care of your baby, be sure to keep all medicines out of reach. This may be inconvenient, but we're all apt to be less careful when we're sick.

Lock up all bathroom cleaning supplies: Get them out of
reach! Don't rely on cabinet locks in the bathroom. Not everyone will be as careful as you to close doors. Visitors, cleaning people, and relatives could accidentally leave doors open and thus expose a curious child to danger. Abrasive cleansers, disinfectants, shower and tile cleaners all contain deadly chemicals. Lock up:

Tile cleaners
Disinfectants
Bowl cleaners and brushes
Ammonia
Air fresheners
Soap powders
Automatic toilet bowl fresheners

Make sure all bathroom outlets have safety caps.

Bathtub fun and good safety habits: Enjoy bathtime with
your baby — climb in there! Kids love company and water play. You don't

need a lot of expensive bathtub "toy centers"; most parents soon find the baby's favorite toy is an empty plastic shampoo bottle. Before bathtime:

▶ *Inspect your bathmats and carpeting.* Be sure your rubber backing is in good shape and skid-proof. Check for fraying edges or tears which could cause an accident. Assemble all your supplies before getting into the bathtub. Lay a thick cotton towel on the floor before you get in, and pop your baby on it to get out safely. *Don't ever try to climb out of a tub while holding your baby.*

▶ Put rubber appliqués or mats on the bottom of the tub to prevent slipping.

▶ Check your shower stall doors to be sure that they can't close on the baby — and be sure shower curtains are kept clean and away from the baby's grasp.

▶ Always check the water temperature before putting your baby in the tub.

▶ When the baby is young, support his or her upper chest with your arms at all times; this will prevent spills which might make him or her afraid of baths.

Never leave your child alone in the water — not even for a second! Babies can drown in one inch of water, as they do not know to pull their heads up from water.

Things That Make Good Bathroom Toys for Kids
    Empty, well-rinsed plastic shampoo bottles
    Paper drinking cups
    Hairbrushes with soft bristles
    Washcloths
Things That Make Terrible Bathroom Toys for Kids
    Empty medicine bottles (baby will think all medicines are toys)
    Toothbrushes
    Hair dryers
    Old cosmetics
    Bathroom drinking glasses

Bathroom locks: Check now to be sure that bathroom locks can be opened *from the outside by an adult*. If not, tape the bolt to keep it open, or

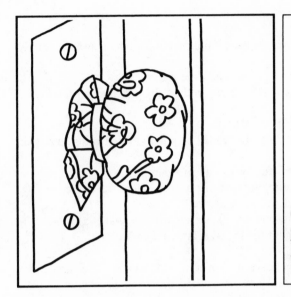

Cover your bathroom doorknob with a piece of fabric and a rubber band. An adult can turn the knob, but a child cannot.

remove it entirely. (If you want to maintain your privacy and keep your locks, place a key on a hook outside the door to open in case of accidental lock-in.) Install hook-and-eye latches high on the outside of the door to keep bathroom off-limits or install plastic doorknob covers (available in hardware stores) that make it very difficult for your baby to turn the handle. (You can make one of these at home by covering the doorknob with a piece of fabric fastened with a rubber band.)

Scalding water: Lower your water heater thermostat now; if your curious toddler turns on the hot water, he or she won't be scalded. If you live where you can't control water heater temperature, exercise caution during all of your baby's bathtime. (If your hot water system undergoes dramatic change due to external conditions, such as flushing toilets, fill up the tub first. Don't allow tap water to run on the baby.) As children get older, they can be taught the difference between hot and cold controls.

Using electric appliances safely: Most children will not leave their parents alone in the bathroom. As it's very easy to get distracted, remember:

▶ Never leave electric appliances plugged in. Put them away promptly after each use.

▶ Don't use electric appliances in a wet room.

▶ Don't use electric appliances when the baby is in the bathroom.

Tips for safe toilet training

▶ Don't leave your child unattended on a potty, whether it's on a chair or the toilet.

▶ Be sure potty seats for toilets have a secure fit.

▶ Always place a stool in front of potty to reduce the chance of falls and teach your child independence.

▶ Always take the telephone off the hook before going into the bathroom so you're not called away from your child.

Bathroom Note: Always leave the toilet seat down – it's safer and more hygienic, and the toilet will not get clogged up by an eager young toilet-paper user.

Baby's room and play spaces

Whether they're the size of a ballroom or an alcove off the living room, all baby spaces need safe furnishings. Before you buy or borrow, evaluate the following features.

Cribs: Cribs today have strict safety standards. When considering any crib (new, old, or antique), always look at these elements:

▶ *Slats* – rounded with smooth edges, no more than $2\frac{3}{8}''$ apart to prevent the baby from wedging its head.

▶ *Locks* – babyproof mechanism with two releases to prevent a toddler from lowering the side. Single drop side is best as it lessens the options for accidental opening.

▶ *Metal hardware* – smooth with no sharp edges.

▶ *Mattress* – close-fitting to prevent a baby from wedging its head. Most parents prefer a foam mattress as there are no inner springs

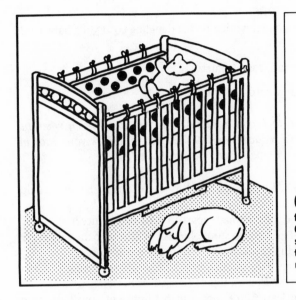

Crib mattresses should fit snugly into the crib. Check railings for splinters and make sure the catches are easy to use.

to break from the wear and tear of an active toddler. Also, some babies are allergic to mattresses filled with animal hair.

▸ *Bars* — run from side to side under crib.

▸ *Weight* — solid enough not to be pulled over.

▸ *Bumper pads* — use fabric-padded bumpers around sides of the crib to cushion and protect the baby's head; vinyl often tears. Pads must tie in at least six places; trim ties to minimum length so your baby cannot choke on them. Remove bumper pads once the baby can step up on them, as they provide a stepping stone out of the crib.

▸ *Construction* — sturdy (you don't want it to rattle at night!).

▸ *Height* — to prevent the baby from falling out, top of lowered side must be at least 9″ above mattress support at its highest position.

▸ *Teething rails* — not brittle or likely to splinter when gnawed by a teething baby.

▸ *Test locks and rail closings before buying.* If a crib is difficult to use, don't buy it.

▸ *Avoid decals* that might peel and the baby could eat.

▸ *All surfaces must be splinter-free.*

WHERE TO PLACE CRIBS

Away from lamps and anything with a dangling cord your baby could yank

Away from windows, fans, heaters

Away from window cords or drapes

Make it a habit always to keep the side of the crib raised, even when the baby is not inside. You'll reduce chances of forgetting to lock your baby in, and help protect young climbers from scaling this height.

Changing tables: When acquiring this useful piece of baby equipment, look for:

- ▶ *Stability* — Are legs far enough apart to provide balance?
- ▶ *Convenience* — Is it easy to store objects? Will your baby pull everything out? Is it high enough for you to use comfortably?
- ▶ *Safety* — Can your baby climb up on it? Fall off accidentally? Catch fingers in drawers? Pull on top of himself or herself?
- ▶ Are the sides at least 6 to 8 inches high to prevent your baby from rolling off?
- ▶ Store powders, ointments, diapers, toilet paper, safety pins out of your baby's reach. Throw away diapers as you use them. If you use cloth diapers, be sure your baby cannot pull the lid off the diaper container. Keep the container closed at all times.

Never leave your baby alone on any surface from which he or she could fall or roll off — this includes beds, changing tables, and sofas.

Don't allow your baby to play with cornstarch powder, baby powder, or talc (or their containers). These substances can be harmful if swallowed.

Toy storage: Open-plan toy shelves are best; the child can see his or her toys and eventually learn to put them away.

- ▶ Place heavy toys on the bottom shelves so they can't fall on the baby when being removed; these include boxes of blocks, trucks, musical toys, etc.
- ▶ Messy activities (paints, crayons, modeling clay, felt-tip markers)

Toy chest lids should be cushioned to protect your child's hands. Remove the locks from self-locking chests.

should be on top, away from the baby's reach.
▶ Leave frequently used activities within your baby's reach.
▶ Remember to rotate toys to keep your baby interested.

Caution: Toy-chest lids are heavy and if they slam down suddenly they can crush a child's fingers and injure his or her head. Cushion the edges with foam, foam tape, or pieces of cork; check that hinges are in working order.

Do not use any toy box that is self-locking. Your child could get trapped inside.

Mobiles and dangling toys can provide hours of fun — but be sure they are hung so your baby cannot get caught in the strings. Crib pals should be soft, warm, cuddly . . . and washable! Check that any eyes or buttons on toys are securely attached.

2

Trouble Spots in the Home

Now that you're on the Childproofing tour, look for these trouble spots.

WINDOWS

Every year many young children are hurt in falls from windows; some even die. In many communities it is the law that landlords provide gates for every window above the third floor. Assess your situation now from every window in your house. Ask yourself: Could my child fall from this window? Would he or she be hurt? Safety elements to consider:

▶ Do you have window bars? Gates? Heavy screens? Locked screens?

▶ Is there furniture placed in front of the window that your baby could climb onto?

▶ Are window locks and latches installed away from your baby's grasp?

▶ Do you open windows only from the top?

▶ Are there dangling cords from blinds or draperies to twist around your baby's neck?

▶ Do your floor-to-ceiling windows and sliding glass doors have decals or tape placed at child's-eye level to prevent walk-through?

▶ Do screens have locks on them to prevent your baby from pushing them out?

Acorn locks and other types of window latches are available in hardware stores. Acorn locks fasten on the side of the window frames to allow windows to be opened only to a certain height. Window bars that fit tightly and cannot be pushed open by your child should be considered for every window above the first floor.

Warning about Window Blinds
Some of the new "decorator-type" venetian blinds with narrow rigid slats can give your baby a nasty cut if he or she accidentally falls on them. One child we know nearly lost the tip of his finger on these razor-sharp blinds. Roll them up out of your baby's reach if yours feel dangerous.

RAILINGS

▶ Are they no more than 2⅜″ apart to prevent heads from getting stuck?

▶ Are all sharp edges sanded or smoothed?

▶ Are they free from rust?

▶ Are they free from toxic paint?

Install Acorn locks on the sides of the window frame to prevent window from opening beyond a certain height.

TROUBLE SPOTS IN THE HOME

FLOORS
- ▸ Are they non-splintering?
- ▸ Are they non-slippery?
- ▸ Are all rugs on stairs or landings removed?
- ▸ Are all cracks or tears in linoleum repaired?

DANGEROUS PLACES FOR FINGERS
- ▸ Doors, especially swinging doors
- ▸ Door hinges
- ▸ Deck chairs
- ▸ Dishwashers
- ▸ Ironing boards
- ▸ Folding tables and chairs

STAIRWAYS
As climbing is one of their great accomplishments, babies love stairs! If you have stairs at home, you must install safety gates at the head and foot of every stairway, but — always remember — your adventurous toddler may soon scale even these.

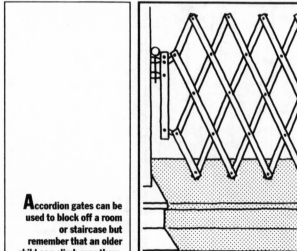

Accordion gates can be used to block off a room or staircase but remember that an older child can climb over them.

Mesh gates fasten with pressure catches. They're best used in low-traffic areas where you won't have to maneuver them with your arms full.

There are different types of gates available at hardware stores and some children's toy stores. We have never found a parent who was completely happy with any of these; each type seems to have its pros and cons.

Accordion gates: These collapsible wooden gates are permanently attached to one side of the opening and latch onto a closure on the other. They are sturdy, but very small children could catch their heads in them. Also, they are easy to climb . . . a factor to be considered as your baby grows.

Pressure bar and portable mesh gates: Both secure to walls through pressure catches, thus allowing the possibility of their being pushed out (admittedly by a very strong baby). They are not very convenient to use when holding a baby.

When installing gates leave three or four steps open for children to practice climbing. (Many parents encourage babies to crawl downstairs backwards to prevent falls.)

To prevent accidents:
> ▶ Keep stairways brightly lit at all times.

TROUBLE SPOTS IN THE HOME

- ▶ Install railings or bannisters on all open stairways (see Railings, p. 33).
- ▶ Cover stairs with padded nonskid carpeting if possible. Check that carpet tacks are firmly in place.
- ▶ Check all stair coverings regularly for worn spots or holes that you or your baby could trip over.
- ▶ Never let clutter accumulate on stairs.
- ▶ Never play on stairs.
- ▶ Don't allow toys to pile up on stairs.
- ▶ Don't show your baby that sliding on the bannister is fun!

DOORS

- ▶ Beware of doors that slam shut and lock automatically, leaving your baby inside and you out.
- ▶ Be sure doors can be opened from inside and out.
- ▶ Test to see that the baby cannot catch fingers on hinges.
- ▶ Wedge doors open that could slam shut on the baby if there is a sudden draft.

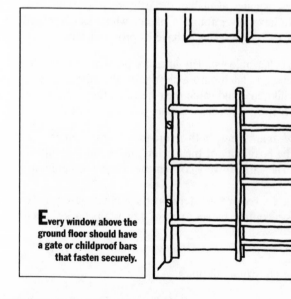

Every window above the ground floor should have a gate or childproof bars that fasten securely.

▶ Remove heavy metal door stops until the baby is older and not likely to be attracted to them.

Beware of swinging doors from kitchen to dining room or wherever — they're a menace.

Sources of heat:
We don't have to tell you that everything possible must be done to prevent your child from being burned. Here are common areas of potential danger from which you should shield an active baby.

FLOOR REGISTER GRATES
Usually found in older houses; your baby should be kept away.

FIREPLACES
Never leave your baby alone by a fire — not even for a second! Always cover fire with a secure screen that cannot be opened or pulled down by your child. If you have a glass enclosure, be sure that it is heat-resistant to touch. Be sure there are no holes in screen for sparks to fly through.

▶ Don't try to start a fire if you are alone with the baby.

▶ Check that anvils, stokers, brooms, and shovels are not tipsy or within the baby's reach.

▶ Check that wood and kindling are stored in such a way that they cannot topple over on your baby or give him or her splinters.

ELECTRIC HEATERS
If you must use them, keep well out of your baby's reach. Be sure cord is away from the baby's sight and grasp.

Never use kerosene heaters — they are too dangerous around young children.

WATER HEATERS
Never allow your baby near the open flame of a gas water heater. Also, check for insulation; heater should not be hot to the touch.

RADIATORS
Enclose all radiators or block them from your baby's reach.

Install fire alarms and smoke detectors in all rooms.

WHOM TO CALL FOR HELP

Fire Department
Post the telephone number of your fire department next to every phone in the house. In many communities, local fire departments will visit your home to inspect for safety, giving you good advice on emergency procedures, lines of exit in case of emergency, and ways to eliminate fire hazards in the home. Obtain "tot detector" decals from the fire department; these decals will alert firefighters to the presence of children in your home.

Never leave your baby alone in a room with a lighted cigarette, cigar, or pipe. You might be called away and forget about it.

- ▶ Never leave lighters or matches lying around.
- ▶ Don't be afraid to ask guests, relatives, or babysitters not to smoke near your baby – or *not at all* if you're not home.
- ▶ Never leave cigarettes where your baby can reach them. The nicotine in tobacco can make your baby ill if he or she chews it.

Place reflective "Tot Detector" decals on the windows of your child's room and outside entryways to alert the fire department in case of an emergency.

ELECTRICITY

We don't exactly know why young children, especially babies, are drawn to electrical outlets, cords, and switches, but they are. Here are several protective measures:

- ▶ Fill all empty sockets with plastic caps available in hardware stores.
- ▶ Replace worn cords.
- ▶ Tape connections between cord heads to prevent the baby from pulling them apart.
- ▶ Tape down cords to prevent tripping.
- ▶ Place furniture in front of sockets.
- ▶ Keep switches in "off" position when not in use.
- ▶ Never leave a lamp or lighting fixture empty—replace bulbs immediately, before your baby can stick his or her finger into the socket.
- ▶ Install plastic outlet covers that prevent children from pulling out plugs by shielding the whole outlet.
- ▶ Fasten excess cord with tape to prevent your baby from playing with it.
- ▶ Do not place lamps where your baby can burn his or her hands on hot bulbs.

3

Poison Alert

When I learned that my child could be poisoned by the detergent I was putting in my dishwasher I decided it was time to learn more about poisons. A review of the following list will make you more aware of the many poisonous substances found in the average home. Each year, many children are accidentally killed or seriously injured by ingesting these toxic substances. Take the time to eliminate these hazards from your home. *Any poisonous substance you keep in the home must be stored in its original container (preferably a childproof one) and kept well out of your baby's reach.* Paste labels on these with the word "POISON" clearly displayed. In case of emergency, you must know what the poison was.

Remember, no matter what precautions you take, your child could be accidentally poisoned. Don't wait for an emergency. Discuss poison control with your pediatrician at your earliest opportunity. He or she will give you specific instructions on what to administer in case of poisoning and where to get help instantly. Many communities and large cities have poison control centers manned 24 hours a day, seven days a week. Next to every telephone post the following numbers:

Pediatrician

Poison Control Center

POISON ALERT

Physician

Hospital Emergency Room

Emergency Rescue Squad

Be sure that everyone who watches your child knows whom to call in case of a poisoning emergency. And bear in mind that it takes only a small amount of a substance to poison a small child.

We also recommend purchasing a good first aid book, such as *Emergency First Aid for Children* by Emily Blair Chewning (Addison-Wesley, 1984), reading it, and keeping it displayed in a prominent, easy-to-get-at place in your home. Discuss basic first aid with your spouse and anyone who watches your child.

What is *ipecac syrup*? You may hear this come up in conversations about poisonings. Be sure to discuss this with your pediatrician. Ipecac syrup can be obtained at a pharmacy without a prescription. It causes vomiting, thus ridding the toxic substance from the body before absorption occurs. It will save you valuable time in an emergency; that is why we recommend that you have it in the house. Keep it away from children, but where adults can get to it fast. *Ipecac syrup is not for every emergency. Do not use it without the advice of your doctor or poison control center.*

POISONS FOUND IN THE HOME – KEEP OUT OF CHILDREN'S REACH

ammonia and ammonia products	furniture polish
bleach	metal polish
drain cleaners	grease removers
oven cleaners	carbolic acids
lye	dishwasher detergents
sodium carbonate (washing soda)	wall cleaners

floor waxes
aerosol dusting sprays
shoe polish
clothes detergents with
sodium carbonate
toilet bowl cleaners
tile cleaners
air fresheners
carpet cleaners
upholstery cleaners
mothballs
ink
cigarette lighter fluid
typewriter cleaners

typewriter correction fluids
model cement
mercury batteries (for cameras,
hearing aids, etc.)
iodine
boric acid
shaving lotions
mouthwashes
hair dye and permanent solutions
rubbing alcohol
aspirin and aspirin substitutes
vitamins with iron
over-the-counter medicines

GARAGES AND BASEMENT WORKSHOPS

pesticides
rat poisons
insect poison
charcoal lighter fluid
turpentine
paints, especially outdoor paint
containing lead
paint remover
paint thinner
turpentine
wood stains
wood preservatives
brush cleaners
pine oil cleaners
gasoline

antifreeze
motor oil
car cleaners
kerosene
benzene
transmission fluid
muriatic acid
glue
sulfuric acid (contained in
car batteries)
rust removers
methyl or wood alcohol
fertilizers
weed killers

When discarding any poisonous substances, always be sure that the containers are empty, rinsed clean, and placed in a covered garbage can where your baby cannot touch them.

Poison plant checklist: So many ordinary plants, flowers, and trees contain poisons which could prove harmful or fatal if ingested by your baby that you should never allow your child to put any part of a plant or flower into his or her mouth. This includes leaves, stems, seeds, bark, nuts, or any part. Below is a list of poisonous plants commonly found in and around the house. Although many plants have to be ingested in large quantities to cause poisoning, call your pediatrician or local poison control center immediately if you should discover your child eating any of these. (Remove the plant from the baby's mouth and keep it for identification.)

When buying plants, flowers, and shrubs, always inquire if they are poisonous. Keep a record of the names of all your plants either on the bottom of the plant or on a name tag or stick.

The following plants have varying degrees of toxicity and can cause symptoms ranging from nausea and vomiting to stomach pains. Some can cause burning and irritation to the mouth and throat. Some can cause death. Keep your child away from all of them. Immediately call for help if you suspect your child has eaten any of the following plants:

Aconite
Anemone
Apple seeds (in large quantities)
Autumn crocus
Avocado leaves
Azalea
Black locust trees
Black nightshade
Buttercups
Caladium
Calla lily
Castor bean seed
Catnip plant
Cherry plants
Christmas pepper
Common privet
Daffodil bulbs

Deadly nightshade
Delphinium
Dieffenbachia or dumbcane
Foxglove
Holly (berries)
Horse chestnuts
Hyacinth bulbs
Hydrangea
Iris
Ivy: Boston, English, and others
Jack-in-the-pulpit
Jerusalem cherry
Lantana
Laurel
Lily of the valley
Mayapple
Mistletoe (berries)

Some common house-plants are poisonous if eaten. Check the Poison Plant checklist for such innocent-looking plants as (*left to right*) Caladium, Philodendron and Narcissus.

Monkshood
Morning glory
Mountain laurel
Narcissus bulbs
Nephthytis
Nicotiana
Oak leaves and acorns
Oleander
Philodendron
Poinsettia
Poison hemlock
Poison ivy
Poison oak
Pokeweed
Potato vines, sprouts, stems

Pothos
Privet leaves and berries
Ranunculus
Rhododendron
Rhurbarb leaves
Rosary peas
Sweet pea
Thornapple (jimson weed)
Tobacco
Tomato plant (leaves)
Tulip
Wild black cherry trees
Wisteria
Yellow jasmine
Yew

4

**Protecting your child's
everyday world**

Safety do's and don't's

Having a small child means constantly being on the alert for potentially dangerous situations. Make life easier for yourself by establishing firm safety habits from the beginning.

Never leave your baby unattended — or in the care of a stranger.

- ▶ Never tie a pacifier on a string and hang around the baby's neck; it could strangle the baby.
- ▶ Never give the baby objects small enough to be swallowed or cause choking. Remember that everything goes into a baby's mouth: buttons, beads, jewelry, coins, nuts, pistachio shells, pills, marbles, poptops, small pieces of fruit or stones from fruit, candy, rubber bands, pieces of puzzles, etc.
- ▶ Never leave small sharp objects lying around: scissors, nail files, etc.
- ▶ Always clean up after yourself before you forget those crochet hooks, needles, thimbles, forks, knives, pens, pencils, hobby tools, and so on.
- ▶ Always dispose of *all* plastic bags immediately, and safely. Small children can suffocate on them.
- ▶ Don't permit children to play or run with sharp objects: lollipop sticks, pens, pencils, pinwheels, balloon sticks, chopsticks, batons,

cutlery, eyeglasses, etc.
▸ Always feed the baby or toddler from plastic cups and plates that can't break.

Children's clothing

▸ Check clothes for tight elastic bands around neck, arms, and legs that can be constricting.
▸ Remove cords and long strings from clothing and caps.
▸ Be sure clothes are not tight or binding in any way.
▸ Check regularly that all buttons are sewn on tightly.
▸ Are you using safety pins? If so, are they baby-safe?
▸ Always check for any loose threads (especially the clear plastic kind) that can get wrapped around a baby's fingers or toes.

NON-FLAMMABLE SLEEPWEAR

Today, federal regulations require all children's sleepwear from infants' to size 6X to be marked either "Flame Resistant" or not. Check labels to determine contents of fiber. We recommend that you buy pure cotton or non-flammable synthetic sleepwear with no chemicals added, and to retain flame resistancy that you follow manufacturer's instructions on laundry care.

Toys

When selecting toys, always consider safety first. Don't assume that all toys are safe. Far from it: most toys are not safety-tested before being marketed. Inspect any toy before purchasing or allowing your child to play with it — that goes for gifts too. You can follow the manufacturer's recommended age group for the toy, but always use your own common sense. A toy that is safe for a three-year-old may harm an infant. Any toy your child uses should suit his or her abilities. For information on hazardous toys, write

Toy Safety Review Commission,
Bureau of Product Safety
U.S. Food and Drug Administration
5401 West Bard Avenue,
Bethesda, Maryland 20016

▶ Check all your child's toys regularly for sharp edges or points, loose pieces, splinters, weak seams, shoddy construction. And be realistic: throw away broken toys you can't mend.

▶ Teach your growing child how to use the toy—and then, where to store it. (This may take a while to accomplish, but most children respond to a sense of order.) See Baby's Room, p. 28.

FOR INFANTS ESPECIALLY

All toys go into the mouth! Be sure they're safe for chewing . . . and washable! Beware of small decorative rattles which can jam in your baby's mouth. (Often these rattles come with floral arrangements sent to hospitals.)

▶ Never give your baby a toy that's brittle enough to break or splinter.

▶ Never give your baby a toy with sharp edges or points, or a toy that is small enough to swallow.

Avoid:

▶ Battery-operated toys; batteries may leak, causing burns.

▶ Toys with long cords or strings that could strangle the baby.

▶ Toys that are easily broken or that cannot withstand rough play.

▶ Toys that shatter when broken.

▶ Toys that are heavy enough to cause injury if dropped on a child.

▶ Toys that are not clearly labeled "NONTOXIC".

▶ Anything with lead-based paint.

▶ Toys with projectiles like dart guns that can injure eyes.

▶ Toys with small pieces.

▶ Toys with wires or spikes inside that could cut the child if exposed.

▶ Toys that can come apart or separate easily.

▶ Wooden toys that are not sanded smooth.

▶ Toys that make loud noises that could scare the baby or damage hearing.

▶ Toys that could catch the baby's hands (jack-in-the-box, etc.)

▶ Dolls with china heads that could be broken.

▶ Dolls with pins or tacks on doll's clothing.

▶ Dolls and stuffed toys that are not labeled "Washable/Hygienic materials."

▶ Dolls with hair long enough for the baby to choke on.

▶ Toys filled with liquid substances.

High chairs should have sturdy, well-balanced legs, a workable safety belt and easy—to—operate latches.

Strollers

Today's umbrella strollers are lightweight and collapsible. Unfortunately, they are not all sturdy, and their aluminum frames can bend and break. For more intense use, think about purchasing a heavy-duty stroller. Look for:

▶ Well-padded upholstery for comfort
▶ Reclining seat for the baby to rest on
▶ Rubber tires to absorb shock
▶ Good brakes on both rear wheels
▶ No bolts or protruding pieces of metal to pinch the baby's hand
▶ Seat belts that work easily for you but not for your baby.

High chairs

Every year many babies are injured in falls from high chairs. Children will use high chairs from the age of six months and up. Your baby will spend a lot of time in it, so be sure your chair has these safety features:

▶ Legs that are sturdy, well-balanced, and set wide enough apart to be tip-proof.

▶ Design that allows you to put in and take out your baby smoothly and comfortably.

▶ Sturdy restraining straps at waist *and* crotch to prevent your baby from sliding out of chair.

▶ If the tray is removable, make certain latches are easy to operate, and that they lock securely and don't pinch.

In *collapsible high chairs*, make sure locking devices are rigid when closed and pose no threat of accidental collapse.

Warning: Don't rely on a high chair tray as a restraining device.

Do not think of the high chair as a playpen. Many children become bored and restless when left for long periods. And never leave your child unattended while he or she is eating.

Animals and pets

FAMILY PETS

It would be wonderful if all babies and animals got along, but sometimes they don't. Don't assume that Rover is immediately going to love Pasquale, Jr. Some family pets adapt while other insist on all your attention. Play it safe and don't leave your baby alone with your pet. As your baby grows, he or she can be taught to be gentle with the pet, and mutual trust can be instilled. In general:

▶ Don't allow pets to sleep with the baby. Protect your baby with netting over carriage.

▶ Keep animal food dishes scrupulously clean and out of the baby's hands.

▶ Keep kitty litter boxes out of your child's reach.

▶ Keep pets free from fleas, which could harm the baby.

WARNING: Flea collars contain pesticides to which it is dangerous to expose your baby. Treat pets for fleas away from your baby.

▶ Keep fish tanks, bird cages, hamster cages, and the like away from the baby's reach.
▶ Never tease your pet with the baby.
▶ Don't let the baby feed the pet.

ON THE STREET
Teach your baby not to be afraid of animals, but to be cautious. Do not approach a dog that is tied up and never allow your baby to pet strange dogs unless you feel certain that the dog is not dangerous.

Car safety

Taking care of your child in a car is a major responsibility. Just as every adult should buckle up for every car ride, small children require special protection. According to the Physicians for Automotive Safety, traffic accidents are the leading cause of death for young children (once they are past the early critical period of their lives). And sadly, many more children are injured in accidents. Don't risk your child's life — *strap him or her in a federally approved car seat for every ride, no matter how short.*

Children's car seats are rigid units, usually molded plastic, that attach to your car seat by means of the car's seat belts. The seats and backs are padded and the child is restrained in the seat by the harness system. The seats provide protection by their design, which distributes crash forces over a large part of the child's body, thus minimizing injury.

Seat belts alone are not safe for small children. A child could be seriously injured in an accident, not to mention the dangerous distraction he or she would prove to the driver. In many states it is now the law that every child under the age of five ride in a car seat.

The worst thing to do is to let an adult hold your child in the car. No matter how much Grandma wants to hold her new grandchild, remember that in the event of a crash, your precious cargo would be the least protected person in the car. The baby's body could actually be crushed by the person holding him or her, or thrown wildly around the car by the force of the collision.

Begin with the ride home from the hospital. Be sure that you have an infant car carrier especially designed for small babies (birth to 17 pounds). These are usually of rigid, molded plastic. Since babies outgrow these carriers quickly, you may want to borrow one from a friend or relative, or purchase the type of car seat that converts from infant to toddler use. Most of the car seats made today have this dual function. Do not put the baby in a small bed on the car seat, as this could topple off if you had to stop suddenly.

Car Seats for Toddlers (20–45 pounds): When we went to buy our daughter's car seat we were bewildered by the variety of car seats on the market. Which would be the safest for us? Since manufacturers tend to provide very little information about their products, other than operating instructions, we decided to do some of our own research. And we started with the government standards.

WHAT ARE THE GOVERNMENT STANDARDS?
The U.S. Department of Transportation upgraded its standards for car seats as of January 1, 1981. Since then all car seats manufactured must be dynamically tested — that is, able to withstand actual test crashes. (Please note if

Choose your child's car seat according to government specifications. Make sure it is installed properly and *use it*, beginning with the ride home from the hospital.

you're planning to borrow a car seat from a friend or relative *made before that date* that it may not be as safe as newer models.) For more information about older car seats you can write to Physicians for Automotive Safety, P.O. Box 208, Rye, New York 10580. This organization also publishes a fact-filled brochure about car seats that features a comparative listing of many of the crash-tested car seats on the market. Send 25¢ to the above address along with a self-addressed stamped envelope.

WHAT SHOULD YOU LOOK FOR IN A CAR SEAT?

Though there are many types of car seats sold, what you really need is a car seat that
1. passes the federal car-safety crash standards;
2. offers a comfortable padded seat set in a rigid frame; and
3. has a strong, secure harness system.

The most crucial part of the car seat is the harness, which consists of shoulder straps, lap belts, and crotch belts. In some seats a shield, which is a protective padded bar, takes the place of the harness. Shields, however, can be tricky. You must make sure that what you are purchasing is actually a shield and not a seat with an armrest or front bar which provides little or no extra protection. Both shields and armrests can be too cumbersome to use and uncomfortable for your baby.

WHAT IS "TETHERING"?

Some car seats come with a strap called a tether. This is an anchor strap that is attached to the top of the baby's car seat on one end and your car seat on the other. All tether straps must be attached to the car itself, usually by a mechanic, in order for the seat to function safely. Remember, the safety value of the car seat is lost if the tether strap is not used correctly. For this reason you may want to purchase a car seat that does not require tethering.

WHEN BUYING

▶ Be sure to try out the car seat before you buy it. Try it in the back and front seat of your car (although the back seat is always the safest). Make sure your car's seat belts are long enough to be threaded through the seat.

▶ Try the harness latches to be sure you can open them.

▶ Make sure the harness is adjustable and, once adjusted, has a snug fit that your baby can't loosen.

▶ Read the instruction booklet. Be sure you understand it. Ask a salesperson for help if needed.

▶ Make sure car seat has a high enough back to protect your toddler.

▶ Make sure seat is raised high enough so that your small, restless child can see out the window.

General car safety

▶ Consider your baby's comfort in hot weather and cold. In summer months, always check the temperature of the seat surface before putting the baby down. Once your baby is exposed to a broiling "hot seat," you'll have trouble getting him or her to sit back in it. On hot days cover the seat with a towel when getting out and remove it upon your return. If it's very cold, bring a throw to put over the baby. (Usually a snow suit will protect a child from seats cold to the touch.)

▶ Never leave a child unattended in the car.

▶ Clear the dashboard and back shelf of all objects that could fly if you had to hit the brakes suddenly.

▶ Keep the car locked when not in use.

▶ Keep it comfortably heated or air conditioned.

▶ Don't encourage your baby to "drive the car" by allowing him to play with controls.

▶ Never leave the engine running when children are in the car and NEVER LEAVE THE CHILD IN A CAR PARKED IN YOUR GARAGE WITH THE ENGINE RUNNING. This could result in deadly carbon monoxide poisoning.

▶ Try not to drive with your baby during heavy rush hours or vacation traffic jams. You'll have enough tension as it is.

▶ Don't drive with your baby if you're tired, ill, or in a terrible mood. You're more likely to make mistakes.

▶ To protect car upholstery from gouges and tears caused by car seats, place a heavy towel under seat.

Yard safety

Now you're outside in the wide open spaces, and you think because there are no open stairways, electric outlets, and hot stoves that nothing can happen to your baby. Look around: there are hazards everywhere, waiting for your baby-safe eagle eye to uncover.

Be sure your child has no access to the road or street, and never allow playing in driveways or roads.

- ▶ Cover all outdoor electrical outlets with safety caps. Turn electricity on and off from a master switch your baby can't reach.
- ▶ Inspect lawn and play areas regularly for broken glass and sharp objects.
- ▶ Never mow the lawn when your baby is nearby; flying debris such as stones, twigs, etc., may hit him or her.
- ▶ Never leave gardening tools lying around. Their sharp or rusty edges can hurt your baby.
- ▶ Do not use power tools when the baby is present. You may be called away and forget to turn off the power at its source or, worse, be distracted and not see that your baby is in danger.
- ▶ Be on the lookout for your baby's attempts to eat grass, leaves, dirt, worms, and so on. Remember, as indoors — everything goes into the mouth!
- ▶ At the beginning of the outdoor play season, check all play equipment for loose nuts and bolts or clamps. Repair any rusty areas and check ropes and chains on swings.
- ▶ Check swing sets, sandboxes, and outdoor play equipment regularly and keep them in good repair.
- ▶ Check your yard to be sure local pets aren't using it as a dumping ground.
- ▶ Eliminate insect nests before they can do your baby harm.

Do teach your child to have fun outside, once you've taken the necessary precautions. Don't be overprotective as your child grows. Children must be allowed to be independent, to make new discoveries for themselves.

Basements and garages

Ideally, these should be off-limits to young children. The potential for danger is enormous. Poisonous substances, sharp tools, and hazardous equipment abound. It's easier to keep the baby away, but, even so, you must set guidelines.

Review this list. Get rid of everything you don't use regularly. Store everything else on high shelves. Lock all poisons in a strong chest or cabinet inside the locked garage. Remember to keep all poisonous substances in their original containers in case of accidental ingesting:

ant traps	acids
antifreeze	wood preservatives
car cleaners	brush cleaners
polishes	methyl or wood alcohol
kerosene	turpentine
charcoal lighter fluids	paint thinners and removers
charcoal	gasoline
matches	paint
fertilizers	stains
strychnine rat poisons	glue
camphor	insecticides

Cover all large and dangerous equipment: lawn mowers, hedge cutters, heavy shovels, snow blowers. Put all sharp tools into boxes that can be locked.

NOTE: Make sure all deep freezes have safety latches on them. Also, close all unused refrigerator doors, and lock them. Or have the doors removed. Children can climb into them and get trapped inside.

Water safety

Today, many parents encourage their young children to learn to swim at a very early age. If you're interested in doing this, we urge you to attend a water safety class at your local YWCA or YMCA or obtain a copy of a reliable book on water safety such as *Watersafe Your Baby in One Week* by Danuta Rylko (Addison-Wesley). You'll learn the basics of water safety and first aid, and most importantly, your child will learn the pleasures of swimming without fear or over-anxious coaching from Mom and Dad. If you have a pool at home or live near one, think about the following safety precautions:

- ▶ Always test the temperature of the water before putting the baby in. Warm water (around 80°F) is usually most comfortable.
- ▶ Never leave your baby alone near a pool — not even for a second.
- ▶ Always make toddlers and infants who have not been taught to swim wear life jackets and vests near pools.
- ▶ Do not allow active running play near water.
- ▶ Don't allow older children to splash wildly near the baby.
- ▶ Be certain your pool is fenced in and protected with childproof locks.
- ▶ Be sure neighboring pools are not accessible to roaming toddlers.
- ▶ Inspect and cover all ornamental pools, wells, and cisterns.
- ▶ Empty all wading pools after each use.
- ▶ Protect your baby's tender skin with a sunblock.

Barbecue safety

Anybody with a backyard usually answers the call to barbecue sometime during the year. While this can be fun, it can also be risky business with a small child—unless someone very reliable is present who will devote his or her constant attention to the baby.

To reduce fire hazards, always grill in a protected area away from dry grasses and shrubs and high winds. Needless to say, keep the baby away from fire, coals, lighter fluids, hot tongs, and so on. Afterwards, *dispose of coals carefully* — don't just dump them on the ground. One mother told us her child was badly burned when he stuck his hand in a pile of still-red-hot embers. Keep an eye out for hot coals when you're in public parks and recreation areas that provide barbecue grills.

Playground safety

Every year, children injure themselves using broken or improperly assembled playground equipment. Of course you have to expect some falls and scraped knees as part of kids' natural exuberance. But before a child uses any playground equipment, parents should check everything over to make sure it's safe.

▶ Look for tightened nuts, bolts, and clamps on swings, slides, merry-go-rounds, monkey bars, seesaws.

▶ Check all equipment for rust or sharp, protruding edges.

▶ Everything should be easy for a baby to climb on.

▶ Sandboxes should be free of broken glass, pop-tops, cigarette butts, debris, etc.

▶ Don't allow your child to go on equipment too old for him or her.

▶ Are toy areas installed over grass, sand, or rubber matting to cushion falls?

▶ Look at the rope swings: are there worn spots?

▶ Are there any hooks on which the baby might catch his or her clothing or skin?

▶ Check sprinklers in playground.

In hot weather, check the surfaces of swings, slides, and other metal equipment that may be too hot for your baby.

▶ Make sure you can extricate your child from any tight spot. In case of danger, injury, or panic, could you get into the middle of the jungle gym? Climb into a dome in the sandbox? Walk up a slide?

▶ Check that swing sets have lightweight seats. Beware of those with heavy metal seats that can really knock a child out should he or she wander behind it.

▶ Are the swing sets firmly anchored to or cemented in the ground?

▶ Watch out that the surface on slides is not so slippery that your child comes hurtling down it at sixty miles an hour. Position yourself so that you can catch him or her in case of fright.

Try to use playgrounds where parents can actively involve themselves in their children's games and activities. Don't just sit on the bench hoping that your baby will get the benefit of all the equipment. Most young toddlers have to be taught how to climb onto monkey bars, how to make a "big cake" in the sandbox, how not to be afraid of the sprinklers. This doesn't mean that you have to hover over your child every second. The happiest kids we've seen in playgrounds are those who have learned how to take risks, accomplish skills, and get along with other children (although this is easier said than done).

Public safety

Kids love to go out for walks, but young children, especially new walkers, are often wild, oblivious of the dangers awaiting them.

Make it a rule that your child always holds your hand crossing the street, until you reach the curb.
- ▶ As time-consuming as it is, always cross with the green light, setting your child a good example.
- ▶ Keep your child's stroller on the sidewalk until the traffic light changes in your favor.
- ▶ Keep your child away from dog debris.
- ▶ When your child is walking along the sidewalk, you should be scanning ahead for broken glass and other hazards.
- ▶ Do not allow your child to touch garbage cans, even though "Oscar" (from *Sesame Street*) lives there.

STORES
Always hold your baby's hand or carry him or her when using escalators, revolving doors, or elevators, or getting on or off buses, trains, or autos.

NOTE: Escalators are particularly treacherous. If possible, hold small children in your arms. Better yet, use elevators — but watch for doors that close quickly. Always supervise your child in crowded department stores. Preoccupied shoppers are not on the lookout for small ones, and will likely trample over them.

Teach your child to ride quietly on buses, trains, and especially in the back seats of taxis. Standing up or jumping on seats is distracting to the driver and can be dangerous.

Never leave your baby unattended in public restrooms. Never trust a stranger with your baby.

Travel and visiting

It's your responsibility when traveling to be sure your baby's new environment is safe. *Never take for granted that other people's homes are as child-safe as yours.* On your arrival, make a quick inspection for all potential dangers, particularly:

> exposed outlets
> sharp coffee-table edges — one of the greatest causes of injury
> glass knickknacks
> open stairways
> windows
> swinging doors
> medicines at bedside

Always supervise your baby in unfamiliar places.

Babysitters

Today, many of us rely on babysitters — either part-time or full-time. For your own peace of mind and the safety of your child, it's important to discuss safety procedures with anyone who is caring for your child. Whether you're having Grandma come over for the evening or hiring a full-time sitter, take the extra time to review your safety routines and precautions. But remember, once you have done this and you have confidence in your sitter, go out — and try not to worry constantly about what's happening at home.

Preparations: First, take a moment *before* the sitter arrives to jot down the following:

> 1. *Where you can be reached*
>   Phone

Address
Name of place or person you are visiting
2. *Your time schedule*
Where you'll be and when
3. *Phone number of trustworthy
friend or relative you
know will be home*

Secondly, it's a good idea to pack a special "babysitter" bag which contains:
1. Spare keys to the house
2. Phone numbers of: pediatrician, parents' places of work, where parents can be reached
3. Spare change for phone calls, taxi cabs, etc.
4. Letter authorizing medical treatment

If the sitter goes out with your child, all she has to do is pick up the bag and go.

Training your sitter: Discuss your basic safety precautions with your sitter. Whether your sitter is a teenager or a grandparent of 12, let him or her know *your* safety standards. If it's the first time you're using the sitter, try to schedule extra time or even a whole session to observe and evaluate her performance with your child. Don't hesitate to point out your preferences such as not letting the baby play with jewelry or make-up kits. Be sure to let the sitter know what's "off-limits" to baby: Dad's workshop, your record collection, fireplaces, etc. Be specific about your preferences.

Tour the house with the sitter, pointing out potential hazards — locked cupboard doors that should never be left open, stairway gates to be closed, dangling phone cords. In particular, take the time to thoroughly review bathroom procedures. If your child is toilet training, let the sitter know what stage the child has reached and how to respond to any mishap. Provide clear-cut instructions on how to bathe your baby, if necessary.

Discuss mealtime routines and let the sitter know how to feed your child (small, chewable pieces of food, plastic plates and mugs). Be sure to explain that you expect the sitter to pay close attention to the baby during the entire meal. Talk about what to do in a choking emergency.

Show the sitter how to strap the baby securely in the high chair, stroller, play seat, and changing table. Explain how to work the locks on the crib, how your baby is put to bed (favorite toys, songs, bedtime routines), and how frequently the sitter should check on your child.

While on your safety tour, point out where the medical supplies are kept (bandaids, antiseptics, children's aspirin, cough syrups, and the thermometer). Talk about any special medication your child may be using at the moment; demonstrate how to administer it safely and where to store it. Write down the name of the medication, the dosage amount, and schedule to avoid confusion.

Hopefully, your sitter doesn't have to be told not to admit strangers into your home, but you might want to point it out anyway. Let him or her know if you're expecting anyone to drop in or make deliveries in your absence.

In general, it's better for everyone if you let the sitter know that you have definite safety standards and rules — and that you expect them to be met. Your sitter is temporarily taking responsibility for the most precious, most irreplaceable treasure in your life. While you may be at work or off on a well-deserved break, the obligation you have to your child never ceases to exist. Make your time away from your child and home as safe and reassuring as your time there.

Emergency situations: We all hope there will not be an emergency while we're gone. However, it's wise to talk openly to your sitter about how she should handle herself in case of an emergency. The main idea to convey is to try to remain *calm.*

Point out your list of emergency phone numbers (placed next to or near every phone). Review what you want your sitter to say on the phone during an emergency situation — age of the baby, parents' whereabouts, exact location of house, and special medical problems. (See Poisons, p. 41 .)

TELEPHONE NUMBERS
Work Numbers
Pediatrician
Fire Department
Poison Control
Police
Pharmacy
Nearest Hospital Emergency Room
Close Relative
Next Door Neighbor

Talk about fire emergencies. Familiarize your sitter with your fire extinguisher; explain how it works and under what circumstances it should be used. Point out your various smoke alarms and explain what to do if they go off. Caution your sitter about eccentric alarms that are set off by cooking, cigarette smoking, etc.

Make sure the sitter knows how to get your child out of the house quickly and safely. Walk her through exit lines — show her if you have a ladder for upper story windows — or, if you live in an apartment building, point out staircases or fire escapes (and caution against using elevators which can trap people in fires). Be sure to indicate where you keep flashlights, candles, extra fuses, and a gallon of water in case of a water emergency.

EMERGENCY FIRST AID
Though it may seem time-consuming, you should review basic first aid procedures with your sitter. Keep a book of easily understood first aid instructions in your home for fast reference. If your sitter is a full-time caretaker, you and your spouse may want to consider going with her to a Cardio-Pulmonary Rescue (CPR) course especially designed for use on infants and small children. These courses teach adults basic lifesaving techniques in case a child should choke or stop breathing for any reason. Many communities offer these courses free or for a small fee.

LETTER OF MEDICAL TREATMENT AUTHORIZATION
When our daughter cut her chin in the playground and required stitches, my husband and I realized the importance of getting medical treatment quickly.

Of course a cut on the chin is not a major crisis (except to the parent!) but if our child had been with her sitter when this happened, she could have been denied medical treatment until the sitter was able to contact us. While some hospital emergency rooms will treat a child without a parent's consent in a life-threatening situation, some refuse to treat minor injuries (cuts, broken bones, etc.) without parent's authorization.

While we don't want to be overly protective, my husband and I would prefer to err on the side of caution. We have given a letter of authorization for medical treatment to our daughter's grandmother and we leave one with her sitter. We have discussed with them the circumstances under which they are permitted to authorize treatment and we have confidence in their judgment. You might want to ask your pediatrician if this is advisable for your family.

SAMPLE AUTHORIZATION LETTER

To Whom It May Concern:

As the parents of _____ we authorize the bearer of this letter to approve of medical treatment for our daughter if it is required and we are unable to be reached. Our home phone number is _____ and work numbers are _____ and _____. Our insurance is with _____ and the policy number is _____.

Our child's date of birth is _____. She is not allergic to any medications as far as we know. Her pediatrician is Dr. _____ and the phone number is _____.

_____

Signed

Creative babyproofing

Now that you've tried to cover all the danger spots and hazards awaiting your child, you're probably exhausted. Remember that no home or environment can be guaranteed accident-free.

Accident prevention is your job — discovering and exploring his or her world is your child's. There will be moments when kids will fall or be hurt. But minor accidents are far outweighed by the rewards of risk-taking.

Accident prevention is also a matter of timing. When you're tired, ill, or out-of-sorts, don't take chances. If you're busy and drained (for example, right before dinner), don't choose that moment to let your baby try out a new toy. Don't push your child if he or she is ill, or when you're in a rush. Just do as much as you can, and then let everybody in the family enjoy themselves — safely.

```
0 0 4 8 5 2 3

CHILDPROOFING  YOUR  HO
ME
STEWART
```